What to Do When You Feel Like Hitting

A No Hitting Book for Toddlers

CARA GOODWIN, PhD

ILLUSTRATED BY KATIE TURNER

CALLISTO PUBLISHING

Copyright © 2021 by Callisto Publishing LLC
Cover and internal design © 2021 by Callisto Publishing LLC
Illustrations © Katie Turner
Author photograph courtesy of Meredith Coe

Art Director: Brienna H. Felschow
Art Producer: Tom Hood
Editor: Laura Bryn Sisson
Production Editor: Jenna Dutton
Production Manager: Holly Haydash

Callisto Publishing and the colophon are registered trademarks of Callisto Publishing LLC

Published by Callisto Publishing LLC C/O Sourcebooks LLC
P.O. Box 4410, Naperville, Illinois 60567-4410
(630) 961-3900
callistopublishing.com

This product conforms to all applicable CPSC and CPSIA standards

Source of Production: 1010 Printing Asia Limited, Kwun Tong, Hong Kong, China
Date of Production: January 2024
Run Number: 5037937

Printed and bound in China.
OGP 16

For Peter,
Eberly, Bobby,
and
Hunter, my
inspirations for
everything I do.
—C.G.

We all have feelings.

Sometimes we feel happy, sometimes we feel sad, sometimes we feel scared, and sometimes we feel mad.

Sometimes these feelings get
big and hard to control.

When these feelings get big and hard to control, we might feel like using our hands to hit someone.

Hitting hurts others. It is not safe.
Grown-ups won't let you hit. Grown-ups
will help you when you feel like hitting.

When you feel like hitting, you can
put your hands on your tummy and
feel your tummy go in and out
as you breathe.

When you feel like hitting, you can wrap your hands around your body and give yourself a big hug.

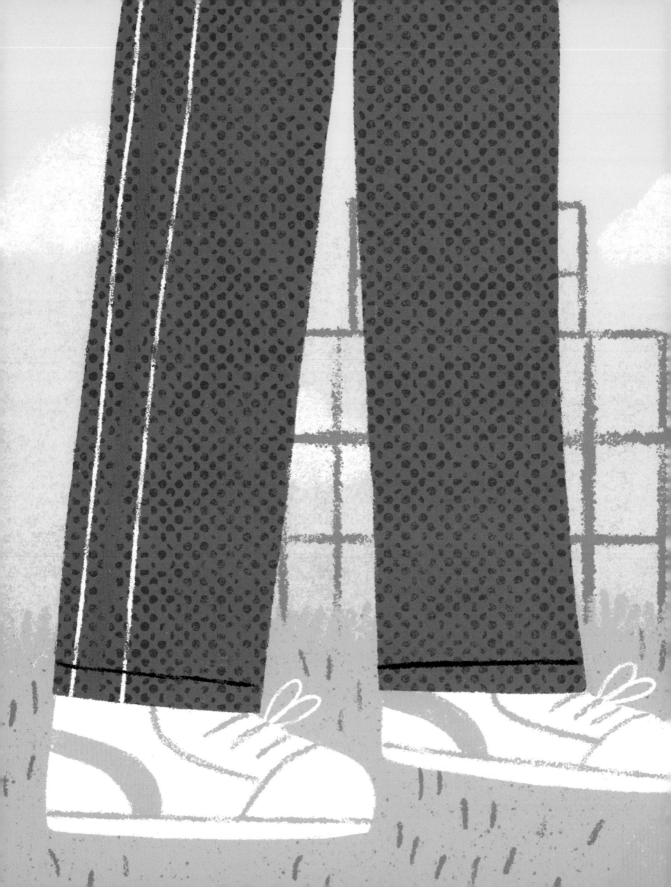

When you feel like hitting, you can raise your hand and say "Help me" to a grown-up.

When you feel like hitting, you can squeeze
your hands into a ball, and then let your hands
go, and then do it again!

When you feel like hitting, you can take deep breaths as you blow bubbles or blow on a pinwheel.

When you feel like
hitting, you can draw
an angry picture.

When you feel like hitting, you can go to a calm-down space.

When you feel like hitting, you can tell a grown-up "I feel mad" or "I feel sad." It is *always* okay to have these feelings.

No matter how you are feeling, you can try to use gentle hands.

You can use gentle hands to let
others know what you need.

help   more

You can use your hands to sign "help," "more," "hungry," or "thirsty."

hungry   thirsty

You can use gentle hands to show others how you feel.

You can use gentle hands to
show others that you care.

love

You can use your hands for many things,
but you cannot use them for hitting.
Hitting hurts, and it is not safe.

I feel
mad.

When you feel like hitting, use your hands to help you calm down and feel better.

It can be hard to learn how to have
gentle hands and calm yourself down,

but you can do it
with practice!

Remember that the grown-ups who love you will always be there to help you!

Hitting is an extremely common behavior among young children, as they have not yet developed the language, social skills, or self-regulation abilities to control their impulse to hit. For nearly all young children, hitting naturally declines as their brains develop and they gain the ability to use more effective strategies. As parents and caregivers, we can help advance this natural developmental process with the following strategies:

1. **Prepare your child for new, difficult, or uncertain situations by explaining what they can expect.** For example, before a playdate you could explain, "We share all of the toys in our playroom. If there are special toys that you do not want to share, you can put them in your bedroom."

2. **Warn your child in advance about any transitions.** It is very difficult for young children to move from one activity to the next, so transitions often lead to meltdowns. To prepare your child for transitions, set a timer and/or periodically announce how much time is left before the transition.

3. **Validate and put words to your child's feelings.** When you see your child becoming dysregulated, get down on their level, look them in the eyes, and help them label their emotions. For example, "I see that you're sad because you want your brother's toy."

4   **Stay calm and set a firm limit.** After you validate their feelings, calmly set a limit for your child. Let them know with your words and your actions that their feelings are okay, but hitting is not. For example, "You cannot hit your brother. Hitting hurts." If necessary, gently hold their hands to keep them from hitting. You can explain, "I will hold your hands to keep everyone safe."

5   **Tell your child what they can do instead of hitting.** Suggest one of the coping strategies described in this book or give them a choice for how to solve the problem. For example, "You can either wait for your turn with the toy or you can play with the blue car instead."

6   **Finally, guide your child to repair the relationship after they hit.** For example, you could say, "Your brother's body and feelings were hurt when you hit him. Can you think of a way to help him feel better? Maybe you could get an ice pack for his arm and then invite him to play blocks with you."

About the Author

CARA GOODWIN, PhD, is a licensed clinical psychologist and a mother of three children. She specializes in child development and has spent years researching child psychology and neuroscience and providing psychological assessments and therapy for children of all ages. Dr. Goodwin translates recent scientific research into information that is useful, accurate, and relevant for parents through her Instagram account, @parentingtranslator, and her website, ParentingTranslator.com.

About the Illustrator

KATIE TURNER earned her BFA from Parsons School of Design in New York City and has been an illustrator for more than 10 years. She particularly loves to draw things from nature, such as bugs, flowers, and animals. Katie is also the author and illustrator of *The Cat Who Got Framed* and *Vanilla Bean*. She currently lives in Nashville, Tennessee.